Dalmatians

ABDO
Publishing Company
A Buddy Book
by
Julie Murray

VISIT US AT
www.abdopub.com

Published by Buddy Books, an imprint of ABDO Publishing Company, 4940 Viking Drive, Suite 622, Edina, Minnesota 55435. Copyright © 2002 by Abdo Consulting Group, Inc. International copyrights reserved in all countries. No part of this book may be reproduced in any form without written permission from the publisher.

Printed in the United States.

Edited by: Christy DeVillier
Contributing Editors: Matt Ray, Michael P. Goecke
Graphic Design: Maria Hosley
Image Research: Deborah Coldiron
Photographs: Eyewire, American Kennel Club

Library of Congress Cataloging-in-Publication Data

Murray, Julie, 1969-
   Dalmatians/Julie Murray.
      p. cm. — (Animal kingdom)
   Summary: A simple presentation of the history, physical characteristics, and proper care of this dog breed known for its spots.
   ISBN 1-57765-642-3
      1. Dalmatian dog—Juvenile literature. [1. Dalmatian dog. 2. Dogs.] I. Title. II. Animal kingdom (Edina, Minn.)

SF429.D3 M87 2002
636.72—dc21

                                                                  2001027927

Contents

The Dalmatian Name

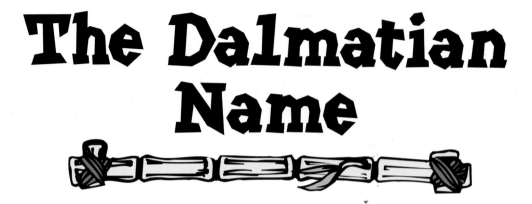

How did the dalmatian get its name? Someone may have named dalmatians after Dalmatia. Dalmatia is a place in Eastern Europe. But nobody is sure dalmatians come from Dalmatia.

Nobody is sure where dalmatians come from.

There was a poet who lived in Eastern Europe 400 years ago. His name was Jurij Dalmatin. Jurij Dalmatin raised black and white, spotted dogs. Maybe someone named dalmatians after Jurij Dalmatin.

Dalmatians Long Ago

Long ago, people used dalmatians as coach dogs. This happened back when people rode in carriages. Coach dogs ran along with carriages from place to place. People could leave their carriage. And the coach dogs guarded it until they returned.

Long ago, dalmatians helped firefighters.

Dalmatians made good fire dogs, too. Fire dogs barked and ran ahead of rushing fire wagons. This cleared the streets so fire wagons could reach fires quickly. Firefighters do not use fire dogs today. But many fire stations keep a dalmatian as their mascot.

What They Look Like

Dalmatians are easy to point out because of their spots. Not all dalmatians have black spots. Liver-spotted dalmatians have brown spots.

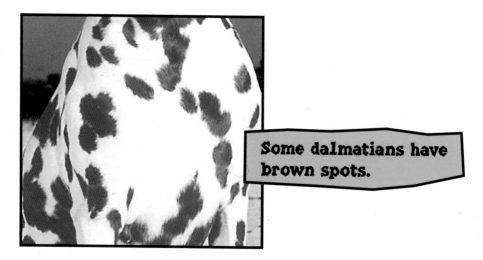

Some dalmatians have brown spots.

Dalmatians are strong and thin. They weigh 45 to 70 pounds (20.4 to 31.8 kg). These dogs stand 19 to 24 inches (48.3 to 70 cm) tall at the shoulders. A dalmatian's coat is short and smooth.

Dalmatians As Pets

Dalmatians are very playful. They can play a long time before getting tired. Dalmatians love running, chasing, and jumping games. A fenced yard is a good place for dalmatians to play and exercise. These lively dogs need exercise every day.

Dalmatians love exercise!

Many dalmatians are house dogs. They cannot stand very hot or cold weather. Also, they love to be around people. Dalmatians like to be a part of the family.

Smiling

Some dalmatians smile. At first, a dalmatian smile may not look friendly. They pull back their lips and show their teeth. A dalmatian may smile to show love. Or a dalmatian may smile after misbehaving, or doing something wrong.

This dalmatian looks happy. Yet, a true dalmatian smile looks different.

Care

Dalmatians are clean dogs. They do not have a strong smell. They do not need a lot of baths.

Dalmatians shed hair. So, you should brush your dalmatian once a week. Brushing removes dead hair and dirt.

Dalmatians like to be a part of the family.

Puppies

Dalmatian litters are big. A litter of 10 puppies is common for dalmatians.

Dalmatian puppies are born without spots. Newborn puppies are white all over. Their spots show up about three weeks later. Around this time, the puppies open their eyes and begin to walk.

Some dalmatians are born deaf in one or both ears. Dalmatians who are deaf in both ears do not make good pets. A veterinarian can test a dalmatian puppy for deafness.

A veterinarian can test a dalmatian puppy for deafness.

 # Fun Facts

- George Washington and painter Pablo Picasso owned dalmatians.

- Adult dalmatians can run for hours without getting tired.

- Walt Disney's *101 Dalmatians* first came out in the 1960s.

- Dalmatians, greyhounds, and whippets are among the fastest dogs in the world.

- Dalmatians may live to be 16 years old.

Important Words

carriage a buggy pulled by horses. People traveled in carriages before cars.

deaf unable to hear or hear well.

litter a group of puppies born at one time.

mascot something to bring good luck.

veterinarian an animal doctor. A shorter name for veterinarian is "vet."

Web Sites

How to Love Your Dog

www.howtoloveyourdog.com
Riddles, facts about breeds, and dog care advice is featured here.

Dalmatian Club of America

www.thedca.org/
Is a dalmatian the right pet for you? Find out at this fact-filled site.

Animaland

www.animaland.org
Learn about pets at this fun site full of games, cartoons, and stories.

Index